D0603029

PRAYING MANTISES

INSECTS DISCOVERY LIBRARY

Jason Cooper

Rourke Publishing LLC
Vero Beach, Florida 32964

PHOTO CREDITS: All photos © James H. Carmichael except p. 17, 21 © James P. Rowan

Title page: This praying mantis in Costa Rica is a twig look-alike.

Library of Congress Cataloging-in-Publication Data

Cooper, Jason, 1942-
 Praying mantises / Jason Cooper.
     p. cm. -- (Insects discovery library)
 Includes bibliographical references.
 ISBN 1-59515-429-9 (hardcover)
 1. Praying mantis--Juvenile literature. I. Title.
 QL505.9.M35C66 2006
 595.7'27--dc22

                                   2005010973

Printed In The USA

CG/CG

Rourke Publishing

www.rourkepublishing.com – sales@rourkepublishing.com
Post Office Box 3328, Vero Beach, FL 32964
1-800-394-7055

TABLE OF CONTENTS

The Praying Mantis

The praying mantis is a long, thin **insect**. It has six long legs. Each leg is made up of joints, or sections.

A mantis may hold its front legs together. Then it looks like it is praying.

The Indian flower mantis seems to be praying.

5

The biggest mantises are longer than your longest finger. Mantises live throughout the world.

Did You Know?

There are almost 2,000 kinds of praying mantises.

The orchid mantis lives in the warm jungles of Asia.

Mantis in the Mirror

What would a mantis see in a mirror? It might frighten itself! It would see two huge eyes on a big heart-shaped head.

The leaf mantis's big eyes almost cover its head.

The mantis would see two **antennas**. Antennas look like little whips. They help a mantis smell. Most mantises would also see two wings.

A mantis's antennas rise above its big eyes.

11

Mantis Food

Mantises eat other insects and spiders. They are the mantis's **prey**. One mantis may eat another mantis.

A praying mantis grabs an assassin bug to eat.

A mantis has little hooks and **spikes** along its front legs. They help a mantis hold its prey. You see, a praying mantis is also a preying mantis.

The spikes and hooks on a mantis's legs hold squiggly prey.

Being A Mantis

Mantises look like the plants they stand on. Green mantises look like green leaves. Other mantises look like dead leaves.

Some mantises look like flowers.

The orchid mantis looks like a flower.

The lichen mantis matches the tree's bark.

Mantises hunt by sitting still. But they watch. A mantis can turn its head in almost a full circle!

A mantis waits for prey to fly or walk by. Then a mantis is very, very quick. It can grab a fly from the air!

This small praying mantis grabs a fly.

A mantis watches for prey.

Young Praying Mantises

A mother mantis lays 100 to 400 tiny eggs in a wet blob. Baby mantises hatch from the eggs. They are called **nymphs**.

A mantis nymph does not have wings.

The ghost mantis looks like a dead leaf.

GLOSSARY

antennas (an TEN uhz) — thread-like organs on an insect's head; they act as "feelers" and help an insect smell, touch, and hear

insect (IN SEKT) — a small, boneless animal with six legs

nymphs (NIMFZ) — a young stage of life in certain insects, before they become adults

prey (PRAY) — any animal caught and eaten by another animal

spikes (SPYKZ) — thin, sharp objects, like nails

*An African praying mantis
with a grasshopper*

INDEX

Further Reading

Brimner, Larry Dane. *Praying Mantises*. Scholastic, 1999

Frost, Helen. *Praying Mantises*. Capstone, 2001

Websites to Visit

http://www.insecta-inspecta.com/mantids/praying/

http://www.desertusa.com/mag00/dec/papr/mantis.html

About the Author

Jason Cooper has written many children's books for Rourke Publishing about a variety of topics. Cooper travels widely to gather information for his books.